LONDON CALLING

Lynne Crockett

First published in Great Britain in 2011 by Lulu

www.lulu.com

This book is a work of non-fiction based on the life, experiences and recollections of the author.

ISBN: 978-1-4466-2134-9

To Liz

No Room at the Inn...

Or in our case at the hospital. Oh joy! But these were not tidings of great joy. It's not Bethlehem, but Bloomsbury. Not as bad as you may think but not when you haven't come prepared, which we hadn't. Well, Liz hadn't. I had my case, I was alright. But Liz had no case and therefore no make-up, no hair product, no PJs, no proper stuff. Not good.

It had all started so well. We had rung the hospital, as it said to in our letter, 'to confirm bed availability'.

'Hopefully there will be a bed.' was the response.

Alarm bells should have rung then. But they didn't. And we set off, with hope in our hearts and faith in the system.

The train was on time. I love train journeys and we had great seats with panoramic views of the countryside and passing towns. There's a marvellous view of Radcliffe-on-Soar power station from East Midlands Parkway. It dominates that part of the Trent valley for miles around. You always know you've reached the East Midlands when its 6 huge cooling towers loom into view. (You also get a great view of it, especially at night when it's all lit up as you fly into East Mids Airport. But that's another journey...)

On through Loughborough and Leicester - we helped a new university student get off at the right university town - Market Harborough, Wellingborough and Bedford. I always look out for the old Bedford Bricks works with its laid out workers' homes, the old clay pits and chimney stacks, all there in the middle of the country side. On to Luton, all back street houses, and Luton Parkway with its airport. On a wet dismal day, like today, you can see the runway lights and I ducked as an Easyjet plane shot overhead to land. Then, it's the final run in to London, St Pancras. Look out for the Wembley stadium arch and you can actually see the stands from the train. It looks unreal. I must go.

St. Pancras and Somers Town on the right where you can see the community garden - a piece of London not known to many - see Shane Meadows film of the same name. (Delightful, quirky Meadows film and I'm no Barry Norman!) The station, if I'm honest, is very 'New Labour.' It's lost that murky, gothic atmosphere in amongst the shiny bars and designer shops. The trains don't go any faster do they? Well, not the East Mids ones anyway.

We settled on a taxi for the short journey down the Euston Road to the hospital. They don't build hospitals in London like we do in the rest of the country. This one goes straight up some 16 floors and I'm on the 14th. Does wonders for my vertigo but the views are magnificent. Make the most of them as that'll be the last I see of them once the drug is injected.

Now this is where the fun starts. They are expecting us. Good.

'There's not a bed available at the moment.' Oh... 'I'll show you round the ward.' Thanks. 'This is where your bed is...'

An arm waved in the general direction of some beds - all occupied. Hmm...

'You can sit in this Treatment Room.' Thanks.

Time passes.

An increasingly harassed Nurse-in-Charge tries to reassure us a bed will become available and then quickly adds something about a hotel. Oh yes..? The Doctor introduces himself and goes through the usual - well it is for me now - any previous allergies, smoke, drink, weight? And then down to the real business. He wants to know what I know about PDT and says the injection will hurt - a bit. I shrug, what does that mean compared to having your throat cut from ear to ear?

More time passes. There's still no bed.

A student nurse arrives and carries out the usual checks. We have fun finding my blood pressure, fill in the forms and sign consent - consent to having my throat cut open again for a 'trachi', perhaps. I didn't see that one coming. Never mind.

More time passes and there is still no bed and will not be one, we're told. A hotel it will be but the car is back at the station at home with a parking ticket which will run out and we can't remember where the spare key is! They hold no prisoners if you leave your car for more than a minute. We make a phone call to Claire who goes to the house, hunts down the spare key and liberates the car before any nasty attendant can do their worse. Victory! Well that's how it feels!

Injection time and it HURT! Liz said that it looked like thick black tar being pushed through my vein. It has been described as feeling like boiling oil. It was hot and had a vice-like grip in my elbow (I love their music) and up my arm. The intense pain lasted seconds, probably; the after-pain lasted a couple of hours. We then had to wait in the darkened room until it was dark outside.

'You're free to go!' and off we set, with my luggage (not Liz's - she had none!) and a map for the hotel; Bloomsbury Park Hotel, near Russell Square. Now, my favourite author of all time is C.P.Snow. I know, not everyone's cup of tea or the usual response - 'never heard of him.' Never mind, I'm sure one of his books is centred around some goings-on in Russell Square; I can't remember which one but old men with white hair, afternoon drinks, murder and the judiciary are all evoked by the name. I'll have to root out the book when I get home and read it again.

It's 8.30pm (ish) and we get to the hotel. Our unspoken fear that they wouldn't be expecting us is unfounded and a room is ready and waiting. We'd had Claire and Mike researching the hotel on the internet and it was fine, just like TripAdviser had promised! Comfy beds, en suite, flat screen TV and room service. Liz had a midnight feast of beans on toast, the cheese board and a pot of tea. I had a Fortisip.

24 September 2010

A Comedy of Errors...

Or so it seems right now. Liz finally made it to the station to wend her weary way when... the bloody train was cancelled! I kid you not. She's text to say she's on one now. I just hope she got a seat and there is a taxi at the other end. The house will probably be full of squatters and Ed Milliband will be the next leader of the Labour Party! Stranger things have happened...

The day had dawned beautiful and sunny, too sunny for me when you've been pumped full of Foscom (for that is the name of the 'tar' I was injected with the day before.) It's super, super light sensitive, which is great for the treatment purposes on Tuesday but not so great when it can cause severe burning even in daylight, never mind the sun!

So, off I trot to breakfast, well a pot of coffee, and to watch Liz eat breakfast (there is no black pudding on the menu. You can tell we're down south! Don't get me started on meat and potato pies!) I go incognito and what fun, apart from being bloody hot, it is! I've got my middle eastern-looking scarf wrapped around my face and my baseball cap pulled on low, slouched in a corner out of the daylight. The poor bloke at the table next to us couldn't eat his breakfast fast enough! The waiters and waitresses didn't bat an eyelid between them. What training! Mind you, this is London and they'll have seen it all before.

We ring the hospital as we were instructed, to 'confirm bed availability' and, once again, we hear the refrain, 'hopefully there will be a bed'. It's amazing how quickly you become cynical. Even so, Liz flags down a taxi and one stops immediately, we leap in, arrive at the hospital, leap out and I bang my head on the roof of the taxi! Fortunately my sun glasses mask the tears and we're soon back on Floor 14, ensconced in our darkened room.

Time passes.

There is a bed! It'll be ready in an hour or two. We'll see.

Time passes.

'You've got visitors!' says a nurse.

And indeed we have. My best friend from school, well, it's her brother and his wife. We've only seen each other maybe once since university days and we all still recognise each other! How amazing and how lovely. Sanity in this surreal world. They were passing by, visiting their daughter and thought they'd drop in to say hello - as you do.

Time passes.

There IS a bed!

Liz is refusing to leave until she sees it and she does. It's more than a bed. It's a room with en-suite. It's bigger than last night's hotel room! It's great. I'm so overcome I'm speechless and Liz thinks I've had a 'turn'. We unpack. We re-arrange the furniture. I settle in - I should have brought some posters. The room is sealed from daylight. Blinds are drawn; large black plastic bags are stuck to the walls to cover any gaps. It's just like black out London in the Blitz all over again. How appropriate with all those Battle of Britain ceremonies last week. I watched a programme on the role of women pilots in WW2 last Saturday. Certainly beat X Factor!

And then, the text to say the train has been cancelled! We should have known, we just should have known. The one bit of good news for me was that it meant Liz had got to the right station and platform and the right train had been cancelled! It makes sense to me.

The room got darker and darker. My allocated nurse did not appear. I didn't mind. I'm too busy texting. Claire, Angela, Mike, AnnMarie and Laura. Everyone needs updating on what's going on.

Time passes quickly now. I decide to construct the longest nonsense sentence by text to Mike! My kind of bonkers fun. Bonkers is something I'm becoming particularly proud of. I might explain at some point.

Liz texts. She's home, safe and sound. No taxis at the station but I'm really not surprised anymore and nor is she. This comedy has become our way of life now, we don't mind any more. Bring it on, do what you want, see if we care!

And so to bed.

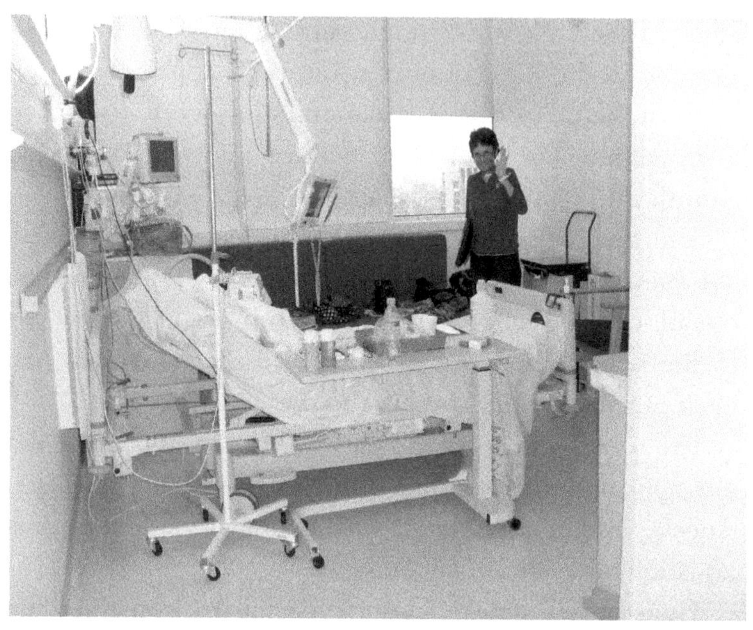

25 September 2010

Fawlty Towers

Early evening and a lovely cup of coffee is delivered to my room. Room service, you can't beat it! It hadn't been that straight forward during the day though.

Dawn doesn't exactly break when you're living in 'blitz' conditions. It does come in other mysterious ways though; like 2.30 in the morning when a nurse arrives to do your blood pressure, temperature etc. Why? And then again at 6.30am; however not before your overhead TV or radio has switched itself on all by itself! Bizarre.

Not to worry, falling back to sleep is not a problem and proper day dawns at 9.20am. I'm left to my own devices, which is fine but a nice cup of coffee would be lovely. None materialises. Never mind I'll listen to some radio on my phone. Guess what, I can't get Radio 4 and I'm right next to the BT Tower! You can reach out and nearly touch the bloody thing but its signal can't reach out to my radio!

Never mind. Eventually the door flies open and I'm out of bed before I know it. It's bed changing time. Now this is a big downside to having your own room. I became quite the little expert at having a lie in when in hospital in Derby. You can see them coming and feign deep sleep even with mayhem going on around you, or put on the pathetic look and say 'not just yet', or my favourite one, 'it's the weekend and I'm having a lie in!' They all worked.

This one's going to take some figuring out here. The old cockney accent can be quite intimidating at first when you're not used to it.

Still I managed to get a cup of coffee out of the visit and an explanation that the, 'TVs come on of their own accord.' No-one knows why and no-one knows how to switch them off! 'It will switch itself off!' It had better not bloody happen between 12 and 2pm, I've got TalkSport on for the Utd v Bolton game!

'Internet connection?' I ask,

'Don't know.' was the reply. 'Have a go, just don't blow yourself up!'

I love it! This is not a hotel, I know that, but it has got some of the features of that fictional hotel in Devon going for it.

A lovely visit from Laura and Harry, who come bearing the gift of an Independent on Sunday. Laura's 'bump' is getting to be quite noticeable now. She has to wear maternity clothes. How exciting. Harry has a go at trying to blow the place up but with no luck. I am to be without internet! Even the internet connection on my phone has given up the ghost... so much for BTFON and BTOpenzone...

What was I promised? 'We'll find the hot spots!' Well how much bloody hotter is this spot? I'm in the South Tower of UCL, right next to the BT Tower! Say no more.

A nice cup of coffee would be lovely.

My room was cleaned this morning and suddenly the cleaner reappears; the fridge, which I thought was for medicines, is found to be full of the previous occupant's goodies. These are removed and a nurse asks if I've had a cup of coffee and says she will bring me one. How lovely.

I read the paper, the whole of the main news section and a good part of the sports section.

'Did anyone bring you your coffee?'

My face tells the answer and it is brought! I'm then asked for more details about myself and suddenly I feel like I'm beginning to belong. This really is one weird experience. I haven't got a contagious disease but it feels like I have. The sign on the notice board says it all,

> 'This single room may be required at any time for a patient who has an infection to be nursed.
>
> This means you may be required to be transferred to a ward bed.'

And it's signed, not by one, but three Divisional Senior Nurses!

How scary is that? It's no wonder staff avoid you like the plague. But things are on the up and an unsolicited cup of coffee appeared early evening, like I said. I suppose the doctor might pop in yet. He did last night, at 11.20pm. He better not turn up during Match of the Day. The TV's still on! I might watch the Gavin & Stacey outtakes on BBC 3. Seen it before but it's a good laugh and I like a good laugh. Bet Liz is watching the X Factor. I'll text. She is!

Now the bloody TV has switched itself off!! Just like they said it would. Just when I'd decided to watch something! It's alright but I can't read my books in this light! I'll just have to find someone to text and annoy on a Sunday evening. I'll be popular. I could watch a DVD. I could play some games on the laptop. I could always try and get another cup of coffee. That usually passes the time.

Maybe, I'll just go to bed.

26 September 2010

The Light & The Dark

(With Apologies to C.P.Snow.)

I didn't go straight to bed. Instead, I had a stupid but amusing hour's worth of text exchanges with Mike. He was in the pub and kept me updated with the World Snooker Final. We had both enjoyed Ronnie's cheeky maximum break earlier in the week. He lost the final; (Ronnie not Mike).

Now the Barnsley & Derby Associates Bonkers Club (B&DABC) has been in existence for 2 to 3 months. It's one of those things which came from nothing and has grown in the fertile imaginations of people who are truly bonkers. People who have embraced it without question; understand its core values without even knowing what they are; have the vision without ever having seen it; give it their all without having a clue why.

Dot is a friend and lives in Barnsley. I live in Derbyshire. I emailed her and suggested she wear a cycling helmet whilst at work and to say she was training to be an astronaut when challenged by work colleagues! As you do. And why not?

B&DABC just grew from there. We have membership cards, headed notepaper, Astronaut Training Certificates (Barnsley the Final Frontier), recommended astronaut helmets (Official Supplier - Halfords[1]).

---

[1] This is purely for creative purposes. Halfords have no link with B&DABC!

We have an Honorary President - Desdemona; a donkey. She lives in Skegness but has had some great adventures. She is currently in Tobago, sampling the delights of the place in readiness for our annual conference there. Why there? There is a hotel with Bonkers as part of its name (Toucan & Bonkers) - an obvious location. Capital, Scarborough - you couldn't make it up! She's training her donkey cousins for transport for our Gala Dinner (Special Guest: Dizzee Rascal. Who else?) A special delegate's pack has been prepared.

We have an Official Grocer to the Club. Mike (he works for the Co-Op. Obvious choice.) He's responsible for the pop and crisps for our meetings and day trips (the National Space Centre naturally and the Kicking Donkey pub in Somerset). We have a trainee Trainer, Liz (she spotted the potential of the BT Tower for astronaut training purposes). She's now the Club's secretary.

So my trials and tribulations with BT and lack of a signal led to some off the wall text banter with Mike. And B&DABC's first campaign had been born before we knew it. We needed a slogan and posters; the following were devised (well pinched really):

- A BT Signal is for Life Not Just for Xmas
- Your Country Needs a BT Signal
- BT Signals, You Know They Make Sense
- Go To Work on a BT Signal

- A Signal Helps You Work, Rest and Play
- Freedom is a BT Signal
- Stay Calm and BT Carry On
- To BT or not BT
- BT is the Signal of Our Discontent

We like the last two best and our chosen method of communication will be Signal Radio!

Oh, and our chant will be, 'What do we want?' 'A BT Signal', 'When do we want it?' 'Now!' Say no more.

My room has had the light meter treatment this morning. I'm allowed more and more light each day. (Artificial. Natural is still too dangerous.) So a nurse - very much like a cricket umpire, solemnly used a light meter to check for brightness as though the Ashes depended on it. The bed side light is now deemed to be safe. I can read during the day now, hopefully at night too. (Michael Mansfield - Memoirs of a Radical Lawyer. A cracking good read.)

I'm so pleased to be reading again. I love my books. Holidays would see me filling the suitcase half full of them. Our back bedroom is my library really. And yet I lost the ability to concentrate on reading books. There's probably some psychological or physiological explanation for it all but it doesn't matter, I can read again. One of the dark episodes of this illness I suppose.

The B&DABC campaign must be having some effect. I can pick up Radio 4 on my phone's radio app. I have a signal of some sort! There is light!

I have been complimented today. The lovely cleaner was overjoyed at my clean and pleasant room. I can come again! Hope not! Student nurse has just been in (blood pressure checks, obs). She watched some PDT ops on Friday! Everyone is so positive about the process. My cleaner - who's name I didn't catch (damn hearing!), was saying most people track Mr Hopper (the Consultant) down through trawling the internet. I'm so lucky the doctor in Derby knew all about it.

I know this is a hospital but why do folk keep expressing amazement that I'm not on any medication? Not even pain killers! This will all change tomorrow no doubt.

My phone is clever because it 'does' the weather. I love it when it rains. Raindrops run down the screen and a windscreen wiper sweeps across to wipe them away, smearing them in the process. It's very realistic. Can't wait to see what it does when it's cold, frosty and snowy. The lightning is pretty impressive too. Anyway, today it was foggy in London according to my phone. I couldn't see the sun it was so bad! A 'proper pea souper.' The kind of stuff Jack the Ripper operated in. Who needs to be able to look out of the window when you've got the technology I say!

It's dark outside now. I know that because the wallpaper on my phone is also clever! I chose one which is lovely and bright and blue during the day and a deep dark blue at night. It passes through a 'sunset' as it gets darker and darker. So, I know it is dark outside now.

27 September 2010

Ginger Nuts

On Radio 4 yesterday evening was one of those comedy programmes that make you burst out loud laughing. Panel members are challenged to sneak 5 silly and stupid truths about their topic past their fellow panellists. Last night's topics ranged from Henry Ford to biscuits. David Mitchell's chairmanship degenerated to such a low point that the panellists decided they had a 'supply' chair and started that horrible humming sound every supply teacher must dread! It took my mind off things.

Why is it that all doctors (male) are crap at taking blood? I can now ask that question with some authority, as I probably wrote about this when I was in hospital in Derby. They just cannot do it. This morning it took 2 doctors (male), 2 attempts in 2 different veins to obtain 3 small vials of blood! It's a good job I'm not superstitious!

I nearly called today's entry The Journey. This was certainly not in any way homage to a certain political autobiography which a former PM has just published. My journey is a proper journey; requiring a mode of transport to get from one place to another. Not some figment of someone's imagination! Getting myself going now, it'll show in my blood pressure checks, I better calm down. So, I didn't call it that.

My journey consisted of lying on a hospital trolley covered from head to foot in a blanket! I couldn't see a thing and no-one could see me! I had protection from the light again - all the way into the anaesthetic room. How very strange. Hospitals are public buildings and you see folk being taken all over the place in wheelchairs and on trolleys. I would have loved to have seen peoples' faces as I sailed past. Even better when I spoke! I would have loved to have seen where I was going!

I had met the anaesthetist and her assistant earlier when they had come for the pre-op visit, together with all the other doctors. She was very direct and was almost certain I would have to have the dreaded 'trachi' fitted... No! I would also have to have the operation breathing tubes down my nose. My airways are very small (just like my hearing tubes) and I would have to be awake while they did this. What a fascinating process - tubes into the back of the hand, then a really big tube down the nose but only after lots of anaesthetising sprays in the nose and down your throat. The Consultant came to look and then nothing.

Waking up in recovery is always interesting. Not as interesting as Intensive Care but interesting enough. I woke at 1.20pm and I had my own nurse. The anaesthetists were there; presumably putting the stuff in to wake me up, then the nurse took over. Sorting out the 'trachi', yes... it's there!

'Couple of shots of morphine?'

'Yes please!'

Dozing in and out of consciousness and then you're deemed well enough to go back to your ward. The Ward nurse was there and off we set - me incognito again! The shroud and her entourage!

Back on the ward by 2.50pm and AnnMarie arrived. I wasn't much company. I spent most of the time asleep. Reassuring to know someone was there. I was flying solo (thanks to Elizabeth for the expression!) almost immediately. No lines attached; just the one needle in my hand for any infusions needed and the 'trachi'. All is well. The doctor had said in recovery that they had located a cancer nodule, remaining from the main op in May, using the light technology and it had now been zapped. And that's PDT. Simple as that and let's hope as effective. Everyone remains positive.

A quiet evening; some texts and what better news to put you on the road to recovery than to learn of Leeds United's heaviest home defeat ever - 6-4 to Preston North End (Fergie's son's team as well; even better!) A lovely text from Angela - our very recently pregnant Angela! The 'bump' it would appear is giving her cravings for ginger nut biscuits. A whole packet in just one day! That's my girl! The last heard was they were all tucked up in bed with a new packet of ginger nuts on standby.

28 September 2010

The Curse of the BT Tower

The day dawns wet - thank you phone. It's windscreen wiper time!

Post-op day and it will be a busy one. There are so many people who want to see you.

First up, Mr Hopper and his gang of doctors; very pleased with yesterday's proceedings - found the cancer nodule and zapped it, just like the recovery doctor had said. 'Trachi' out ASAP and then plan to go home. Yes! He'll be bringing some Italian visitors around to have a look if I don't mind - I don't mind; the more people who know about PDT the better.

Five minutes later and Mr Hopper returns! The room is full, and I mean full, of Italians. Mr Hopper explained where I live, heaped praise on my consultant in Derby and explained about the Light and the Dark situation. I proudly showed my new Italian friends what the weather was like outside on my phone. I think they were impressed! Mr Hopper opened one of my blinds so I can actually see the BT Tower - only 667 days to 2012 and the London Olympics it proudly claimed.

Next up was the physiotherapist and the speech and language therapist. They always hunt in pairs I find. It's 'trachi time!' After much suctioning, letting down of a balloon, coughing and fitting of new bits and pieces I'm back in the speaking world with lots of instructions about what and what not to do. It was all coming back to me. It's still intimidating though. And then it was the turn of the dietician.

'What am I on at home?'

'How many?'

'How often?'

'How do I administer it?'

'How much water do you use?'

We agree on a plan and I will keep a record for the nurses. That's fine. I'm in control of my fluid intake plan.

The pharmacist came next - got to get those drugs sorted!

Dad came to visit. He came on the train - a big adventure. It has been more than 20 years since he's travelled by train! Now, I had a job lined up for him. Hunt down the pay machine and feed it with money so that we can get my TV working for the match tonight (Valencia v Man United in the Champions League). He found the machine. It's not working! I give the BT Tower a filthy look. I am doomed! I don't believe it! It's so unfair!

For once in this technological nightmare, there is a happy ending. Dad has one more go at the machine before going to find a 'little man' who looks after the TVs! He comes and sorts me out! I am with TV. I will watch the match after all. I am a happy bunny!

Then it is 'trachi time' again. This time a cleanup and new dressing. I let an Arsenal fan take a pair of scissors to my neck - I text Mike. He says I'm mental. I know I am! A lovely student nurse has been looking after me all day. She's from Derbyshire! We promise to look out for each other. She keeps her eye on the Arsenal fan for me!

A very pleasant evening passes, although the match isn't up to much, especially the first half. I had a laugh with that Leeds friend of mine. Sent a text saying technically I was still ill and not to be sent related texts which could upset me. I received a response saying this needs a doctor's note confirming it in writing! I composed a text letter from my doctor saying it was very important that I am not unduly upset as I am recuperating and thanking Sue for her co-operation.

Sue's response, 'This is not a doctor's letter. I can read it.' There's no fooling that girl!

So, my £20 for a reconnected TV is not spent in vain and I get to see the highlights of all other matches as well. Why did some of the nurses keep on checking to see if I was ok, couldn't be because the 'footy' was on could it?

29 September 2010

Homeward Bound - it's a Pain in the Neck!

Now I don't want to sound ungrateful or complaining. I'm not. Liz commented last night in a text on the number of times I've had my throat cut this year, well 6 months really. We work it out as three - the full ear to ear job in May accompanied by the 'trachi' cut and then this latest 'trachi' cut. Not bad going for someone who has never been near a surgeon's knife in her life! We reckon my credentials for those pirates' jobs in the upcoming panto season are well embedded now!

'You'll walk the auditions!' Liz text.

I'm hoping it's not the plank!

I know only too well that your hospital discharge is very much dependent on how well you'll manage to cope with the 'trachi' removal. You need to be able to breath for a start!

By-the-way, I've developed my tactic for not being thrown out of bed at some unearthly hour! I don't put the bedside light on - even though I'm allowed to now; instead I insert ear plugs into my phone or radio and close my eyes. This has the desired effect on whoever has been sent to change my bed. They can't bring themselves to disturb me and because I can't hear them coming I don't shoot up in bed when the door flies open! Result! Undisturbed Today programme - mind you it's nearly 4pm now, so this could back fire on me! The clean sheets are here but my helpful helper has disappeared and the bed remains unchanged!

So, am I going home or not? Well, first up this morning was a nurse who had a good look at the 'trachi' and declared his satisfaction with it. In passing, he told me he had heard rumours it was to be removed today. Yes!

Next up; one of the doctors. Very pleased with my 'trachi' progress, out tomorrow. Oh! (I'm still thinking today.)

10.15am - Physio visit. Good look at the 'trachi'. 'Cough', I cough. Advised to keep speaking all the time now and move around more. OK. I can do that. 'Trachi' will be out tomorrow rather than today. No!

11.15am - 'Trachi' Doctor and Head & Neck Nurse Specialist are very pleased with my progress. Not today but almost certainly tomorrow. Okay then.

11.40am - Speech & Language Therapist visit - very positive. 'Trachi' definitely out tomorrow and no reason why you can't go home ASAP after that! Yes! She'd be very surprised to see me here on Monday!

So, am I homeward bound? Yes but we don't know when. Liz is coming tomorrow for a visit.

Does she bring overnight stuff?

What about her rail ticket?

Where would she sleep?

What about hair product?

We've been here before! Let's just 'wing it!'

And in amongst all these comings and goings I've got Claire on the text. I am so pleased to report that I am not the only one with technological problems this week. She got to work today and not only is their network down; they can't get the internet either! It's making that new BT advert all the more hilarious - BT Infinity! I could go on but I won't. 'Kettle on, feet up, it's choccy biscuit time!' was my response to Claire.

Harry visits - a flying visit for one last attempt at connecting the laptop to the internet. A mobile, flash, state-of-the-art 'stick' is produced. I gaze longingly at the BT Tower. It seems to be pointing a finger at me; and; wait for it... Harry met his match!

It didn't work. The bloody thing didn't work. I could weep. I don't. I am going home soon!

30 September 2010

Lovely Day

(I don't have many singles that could be called a record collection but of the ones I do have, this is one. Bill Withers, thank you.)

Well, that's if you can call having stitches and a 'trachi' pulled out of your neck or windpipe a lovely day, but for me it is.

The weather itself is foul, foul, foul; rain, rain and more rain. So bad the Ryder Cup in Wales falls victim to it. All that planning, all the anticipation, all the hype and hope. Sodden. What a shame.

I was woken by two doctors with confirmation that 'trachi' day had dawned. At 10.15am everyone was assembled around my bed and the equipment lay bare. Stitches are cut, dressing removed and out plops the 'trachi' - as simple as that. It doesn't hurt, you don't even feel it. The hole is dressed and that's it, done. I'm breathing on my own, and. No, I don't need pain killers, thank you very much.

It's also confirmed that I'm going home on Monday! I text Liz, Claire and Angela. It's raining up there as well but we're all delighted with the news. Liz doesn't need to pack an overnight bag now. It'll just be a day visit today and she can come and get me on Monday. Sorted! This long distance hospitalisation lark doesn't half present some challenging logistics.

Before I know it, Liz is here! What a lovely day. We catch up on what's been happening. Some post to open. We take some pictures and discuss tales of my op since she left. No tales of the unexpected which is good and then all too soon it's over and it's time for her to go home. I hate goodbyes; but it's been a lovely day.

1 October 2010

Police, Camera, Action!!

Our lovely day did not end as we expected. This should come as no surprise to anyone now.

I'm watching the TV, waiting for a text from Liz, having my own personal action with my feeding tube. I won't go into the detail but at 9.30pm I'm having my bed changed and my lovely clean PJs are looking very sorry for themselves! Liz texts. She's home. Great!

> 'Couple on train 2 seats behind me had terrible row which got quite violent. Was horrible. Anyway, police got on at Leicester n took them away.'

The bloke behind Liz was asked if he would talk to the police if needs be and explained he'd got it all on his mobile phone! Then as she's heading for the car at our station there's a lorry stuck under the railway bridge, making a terrible scrapping sound. Not what you need after all that's been going on!

Still, Carole King and James Taylor in concert on BBC 4 soothe all nerves and it is indeed a lovely end to our day.

Post Script - 1 October 2010

A Room with a View

When we came down to London for my first hospital appointment we went for a walk around the area of the hospital. It's very posh in places. Harley Street is just down the road. There are lovely mews areas down obscure looking alleyways. We looked in an Estate Agent's window. How, nay, who can afford to live round here? Bankers? Inherited money? It's certainly not folk I know. A penthouse for £6million if you please. So, I'm calling my room The Penthouse Room.

Now that I can open one of the blinds not only can I see my old friend the BT Tower but also the London Eye and Big Ben. How much would you pay for my room with a view?

A normal day today. Not much happens at weekends. Usual doctor visit first thing, dressing changed, drugs administered, the usual obs... Radio 4, some old episodes of Time Team then Football Focus and TalkSport for the afternoon matches and regular Ryder Cup updates. USA are ahead.

I've got the internet and my email working on the TV this morning! This is a major achievement for me but it doesn't feel triumphant anymore. It's a bit ponderous but I've done it! I am proud of myself and my perseverance but it still feels like that 'Bloody Tower' won. I didn't get my own stuff to work.

I've had my first outing today since my 'undercover' trip to the operating theatre on Tuesday. If I'm to walk to the station on Monday I need to get my legs going a bit. So, clearance is approved by the nurse and I set off round the ward (there are loads of empty beds today!) and into the lift. Down into reception and into the shop for a paper. Now this is where I get totally flummoxed. The guy in the shop treats me like a long lost friend! He wants to know if I'm now a lot better since I was last in his shop and is delighted to hear I'm going home on Monday!

I have never been in his shop before! Liz has. I haven't. I have a twin! There can be no other explanation, can there? They didn't wheel me in there on my trolley did they?

Last Train to Long Eaton

(With apologies to The Monkees)

The logistics of trying to organise going home on Monday can best be illustrated by an amusing exchange of text messages between Liz and me today.

> 8.07 Liz: 'Going to station later 2 sort out tickets 4 mon. Will let u know outcome.'
>
> 15.43 Liz: 'Hi. I've got the tickets sorted 4 mon. Got guy to explain 'super off peak' times. The 'window' of travelling off peak is between 10am n 3pm. So I could get the 10.30 down n we can get 2.30 home. Or I can get later train down n we get 7.25 home. Sure you would prefer 2.30 but for peace of mind hosp will have to be aware you need to be discharged paperwork etc for 1.30pm at latest. Hope all that makes sense. Oh and reserved 2 seats together for 4 return.'
>
> 16.00 Me: That all makes sense. However, how did u know which train to reserve the seats on for going home?!!'

16.09 Liz: 'Shit! Seats are reserved on 7.25. Never mind if we manage earlier train I'm sure there will be vacant seats at that time on a Monday. Bugger! I thought I'd cracked it n by the time I left tkt office guy looked like he'd lost will to live. Haha.'

Later...

18.17 Me: 'I've had word re Monday but I've to check again tmrw. I think we may be pushing the 2.30 train. But lets c. Nurse is going to try and get folk to get their act together tmrw even tho she won't be here. I'll keep u posted.'

18.25 Liz: 'Ok, as long as I get enough notice. Thought 2.30 might be a push but anyway lets see what they say. Could do without them knowing we have choice of later train coz they might not make such an effort to get you all sorted n out of door for 1.30.'

18.33 Me: 'Too late I told nurse but she said that's a bit late for u getting home so could work in r favour as well!! God this gets so complex!!'

18.37 Liz: 'Makes no diff to me really I'll just get later train down. Just got impression you

> not keen on later train. Hence my grilling man in station to within half an inch of his life, Haha.'
>
> 18.41 Me: 'I will do my best tmwr to try n sort it. Can't promise tho.'
>
> 19.02 Liz: 'Ok. If they can't say 100% def then we'll aim for 7.25 regardless. No use second guessing u.c.l. as we've learnt to our detriment several times already!'

This part of our travel story is set to run and run. I just know it. And I don't know if that lorry is still stuck under the railway bridge at home! But what I do know is that Liz, having mastered the complexities of 'super off peak' is going to have no problem with the offside rule this season!

Ryder Cup: Close of Play - Europe 4 USA 6

2 October 2010

Saturday Night/Sunday Morning

I think I'm so excited at the thought of going home I can't sleep. I have been sleeping really well so far but not brilliantly over the weekend and certainly not this night. I'm also on antibiotics and steroids, the last doses of which I'm not being given until 11pm most nights. I feel well. I feel better than I have in months. I know I'm well rested but I'm sure those steroids are doing something to me (I text Angela earlier and she reckons a 'super buff' Lynne is coming home!) It all means I can't sleep. I get the iPod out. I have tended to use the iPod to take my mind elsewhere over these months and I'm hoping it will take me to sleep tonight.

I don't help myself at all by playing some very lively, very loud bluegrass. It can't be played quietly, I reason. No-one can hear it. I can't sing to it. Well I hope I'm not!

'Tone it down, Crockett!' I do.

Some quieter stuff on the shuffle but it's not working.

Some 'Classical Chill Out', and just as Vaughan Williams' Lark starts to ascend, my drugs line falls out the back of my hand! I buzz for the nurse who strolls in (he is a Chelsea fan. His only redeeming feature is his wife is a Man Utd Fan), smiling and saying he had fully expected it to happen and to find a 'bloody bed!' Charming! It's now 5.40am so he does my obs and cleans things up.

I must finally drop off as I'm woken to be asked if I want my bed changing! Damn! I thought I'd cracked that one.

The good news is I don't need a new needle in my hand and all remaining drugs can be administered via my peg feed. Much better.

A Little Stick of Blackpool Rock

It just gets better and better.

A very quiet Sunday morning - I doze. The internet on my phone makes a sudden and totally unexpected appearance.

'Where the hell have you been?' It doesn't reply...

Why would it? I'm sure that Tower just winked at me. I need to get out of here!

I'm able to follow the Ryder Cup and football matches as they all unfold. And what joy is to be had.

Not only does Liverpool start the day in the bottom three, they are to remain there, after a 2-1 pasting at home to none other than Blackpool!

It's the first time since 19 September 1964 that Liverpool end a top flight match in the bottom three and...

'An unbelievable result for the Premiership new boys, Blackpool... The away supporters go ballistic, the home supporters just go.' I love it!

Blackpool's first win at Anfield since 1967.

Ryder Cup: Close of Play - Europe 9.5 USA 6.5

I've checked with a nurse (as I promised Liz I would), about times for tomorrow. He is not hopeful of a quick getaway and advises us to be on the cautious side. There is a tube strike starting tonight as well which will have knock-on effects. I text Liz and tell her. We'll decide later. She's going out for Sunday lunch. What a treat. We haven't had a proper Sunday roast for many, many months now.

I'm planning a nice quiet evening - new series of Time Team, Ryder Cup highlights, some programme about how England will never ever, ever win the football world cup, Match of the Day and sleep. That's the plan. We'll see.

It's all going to plan so far! All quiet. My Chelsea night nurse is on duty. I'm teaching him the rudiments of Ryder Cup scoring, He checks my blood pressure. We'll get there.

Liz is home. Roast chicken dinner and two puddings! She's getting the later train tomorrow; we decide. We have a plan and we're sticking to it!

2 October 2010 - 3 October 2010

The Sun Has Got Its Hat On...

And so have I! The doctor has been in and it's all official. I'm going home today.

'It is lovely and sunny here,' Liz texts. 'It has got its hat for you.' Yeah!

Once the going home decision is confirmed, your MOT kicks in. they have to be sure you can make it there. So, it's sort the 'trachi' wound, physio check-ups ('Cough', I cough. 'Breathe', I breathe. 'Walk', I walk.) Speech and Language therapy visit, drugs to be taken home, that kind of thing. Phone calls to the District Nurses in Derby. They're expecting me and will visit tomorrow.

It's all coming together nicely - which is more than can be said for the European challenge in the Ryder Cup. It's beginning to come apart. No!

In order to win - with a total of 28 points up for grabs, Europe needs a minimum of just 5 points today from the 12 singles matches. So, we can win 5 matches and win, or win less than 5 matches but draw other matches for half points to make up full points to get 5 points.

It's all very simple really. At the moment (1.15pm), we're ahead in 4, down in 3, lost 2, won 1 and are all square in 2. That's 1 point safe with 9 still up for grabs. OK? Got that? Hope my Chelsea night nurse is following all this!

A Walk in the Park

I had come to London for treatment using this expression when people had been asking me how I was feeling about it. (I had also come with aspirations of spending time strolling around Regents Park, which is not far away.)

Why had I used this expression? It certainly wasn't based on any knowledge or direct experience of PDT; mine or anybody else's. It was more likely bravado. 'I will be fine.' 'London, it is a big place, it knows it all, it will look after me. It cannot possibly be worse than what I have already been through, can it?' It will be a walk in the park.'

The reality is you are not hospitalised for nothing.

When I read back over my first few days here, I seem to be trivialising the standards of care and attention of the staff. They seem 'too interested in my pain killer intake and not interested enough in me.' This is an unfair impression I've created.

This is a hospital and I've been having very specialised care. I didn't need medical care until the day of the operation and ever since. They could have sent me home after the injection. They didn't. They looked after me. I have had superb treatment and care. I cannot fault any of it.

It has been confirmed this morning I'm to come back in 5 or 6 weeks for a follow-up scan and then a week later for an appointment to evaluate how things have gone.

Ryder Cup: Final Score - Europe 14.5 USA 13.5

The internet connection on my phone has disappeared again!

We will get the 7.25pm train home.

24 October 2010

www.ingramcontent.com/pod-product-compliance
Ingram Content Group UK Ltd.
Pitfield, Milton Keynes, MK11 3LW, UK
UKHW020229250726
13967UKWH00001B/274

9 781446 621349